The Light of His Beauty

Recounting the Birth of Prophet Muhammad ﷺ

Illustrated by Rose Paoletti

Adapted by Maryam Qadri

Special thanks to Ghulam Dastagir for supporting this project from beginning to end, Dr. Ghulam Jilani and Shabnam Jilani for contributing to its publication, Shannon Mavi for proofreading the manuscript, Sarah Carreck, our graphic designer, for her personal touch and especially to Rose Paoletti whose artwork brought this book to life and gave it new meaning.

All good things occur in unison.

NURANI KIDS
An imprint of Al-Mukhtar Books

Library of Congress Control Number: 2013946700
ISBN: 978-0-9831488-1-4

Dedication

This book is dedicated to the memory of my late master Hazrat 'Allama Pirzada Mawlana Chaman Qadri – may God sanctify his secret and perfume his resting place (d. 1434 AH/2012 CE). *Al-Fatihah*.

Invocation

From the prayer of Prophet Abraham ﷺ in the Glorious Qur'an: *O Lord, forgive me, and my parents and the faithful on the Day the reckoning is done.*

Preface

Dear parents,

The Light of His Beauty: Recounting the Birth of Prophet Muhammad is meant to be read aloud to your children. It is hoped that this biography will impart a spirit of love and reverence for the Messenger of God and his pure parents. There is a twofold moral in this book: (1) love for the Prophet who is the Light of Allah,[i] and (2) love for his pious parents[ii] which, in turn, teaches children to respect their own father and mother.

The author has endeavored to write this book in an elegant style to help young children build a strong vocabulary, learn how to speak eloquently, and develop listening skills. Since every child enters the world with original innocence, their innate faith (*Fitra*) should be nurtured at an early age. For this reason, *The Light of His Beauty* focuses on the excellence and peerless nature of God's Messenger so that English-speaking children might come to know about his true description and character as well as his miracles which delight, inspire, and astound us all.

The artwork in this book is purely conceptual and is intended to serve as an educational tool to teach young children about the life of our pure Prophet, Muhammad the Chosen. In keeping with Islamic artistic norms, no attempt has been made to create a true to life depiction of a particular historical figure. Any errors found within the pages of this book are the sole responsibility of the author. It would be greatly appreciated if the reader would notify the publisher of mistakes to ensure that such blemishes do not appear in forthcoming editions.

The Light of His Beauty

Recounting the Birth of Prophet Muhammad ﷺ

Nurani Kids

In the Name of God,
the Most Kind, the Kindest

My little readers,

Do you want to grow up to be kings and sages, to grow in the perfection of love? Then listen to a story that the venerable Shaykh 'Abdul Qadir al-Jilani (d. AH 561/1166 AD) – may God be well pleased with him – has to tell, for he is revered to this day as the supreme spiritual helper *(al-Ghawth al-A'zam)* and he wants you to know a tremendous secret about the Chosen One, our beloved master Muhammad ﷺ,[iii] whom God Most Pure sent *as a mercy to the worlds*. You see children, God first created the spirit of Muhammad – may blessings and peace be upon him – from the light of His Beauty.[iv]

ome of you might be wondering aloud, "What does that mean?," or very sweetly asking your parents, "Why?" It means that God is Beautiful and He loves Beauty.[v] It means that He would not have created the world if it were not for our noble master Muhammad – may a multitude of blessings be upon him. But it also means that He loved the world so much that the first thing He created, and blessed, was the spirit of His beloved Prophet of Mercy from among all spirits![vi]

od wanted to lead us out of *the depths of darkness into light*, which is why He first created the spirit of Muhammad from the light of His Beauty. The Messenger of God – may blessings and peace be upon him – is like a shining lamp and a shining sun. He is the sun of the day and he is the lamp of the night! Not only that, but he illuminates. He shines and he gives light, that is, the Light of Guidance,[vii] which was carried from pious backs to pure wombs from the best generation of the sons of Adam, generation by generation, until our noble master Muhammad was born – may blessings and peace be upon him forever and always.[viii]

Our master Muhammad – may a multitude of blessings be upon him – descends from the Clan of Hashim from the tribe of Quraysh. His grandfather, 'Abdul Muttalib, always prayed to God – to *Allah*; and God preferred him over all other men to be the chosen instrument through which the well of Zam Zam was restored. 'Abdul Muttalib – may God be well pleased with him – was further blessed with ten sons, but it was the youngest, 'Abdullah, whom he loved most and who was endowed with remarkable beauty.

There had always been a light that shone in 'Abdullah's face – may God be well pleased with him – but never so much as on his wedding day in the year AD 569, when the radiance that lit his face seemed to shine from beyond this world. 'Abdul Muttalib had chosen Aminah – may God be well pleased with her – to be the wife of his beloved son. And this light, which he carried like his pious predecessors before him passed on to his son, the unborn child in Aminah's womb.[ix]

All the animals of the earth were given the ability to converse on that glorious day; and they exclaimed in one voice: "Tonight God's preeminent Prophet – may a multitude of blessings be upon him – has entered the womb of his mother! He wears the crown of lordship and is the light of the world." Then all of the animals began to glorify God and sing His praises.[x]

wo months later, 'Abdullah – may God be well pleased with him – went with one of the caravans to trade in Palestine and Syria. But on his way home he fell sick whilst residing with his grandmother's family in what would soon become the City of the Prophet – may a multitude of blessings be upon him – Medina the Illumined (*al-Medina al-Munawwar*).[xi] When he passed away the angels cried out and said, "O Lord, Your Prophet – may peace and blessings be upon him – is now without a father!" But God comforted them by saying, "Am I not his Protector?"[xii]

minah's one consolation was a light within her, and one day it shone forth from her so intensely that she could see the castles of Bostra in Syria. And she heard a voice say to her: "Thou carriest in thy womb the lord of this people; and when he is born say: 'I place him beneath the protection of the One, from the evil of the envier'; then name him Muhammad,"[xiii] which means often praised or praiseworthy. May peace be upon you, O Prophet, and the mercy of God, and His gracious favors!

hen little Muhammad – God's peace and blessings be upon him – was born in the Year of the Elephant (AD 570), Aminah again heard a voice cry out: "Let Muhammad possess the features of Adam, the acclaim of Seth, the courage of Noah, the friendship of Abraham, the eloquence of Isma'il, the resignation of Isaac, the gracious speech of Salih, the wisdom of Lot, the glad tidings of Jacob, the steadfastness of Moses, the patience of Job, the endurance of Joshua, the kingly voice of David, the boundless love of Daniel, the chastity of John, and the abstinence of Jesus. Let him possess the brilliance of all the prior Prophets – may God's peace be upon each and every one of them!"[xiv]

hen Aminah – may God be well pleased with her – looked into the face of her newborn son and saw it shining like the full moon!^{xv} This is how the light of our Prophet – may a multitude of blessings and peace be upon him – came into the world for the guidance of jinn and the whole of humanity. As God has said: *There has now come to you from Allah a Light and a clear Book* and *Show gratitude to Me and to thy parents; unto Me is the homecoming.*

Notes

[i] The Islamic Supreme Council of America has recently released *The Muhammadan Light in the Qur'an, Sunna, and Companion Reports* (2012). This scholarly work presents 200 Qur'anic verses and over 250 texts on the Light of the Prophet – may God's blessings and peace be upon him.

[ii] For further discussion of this topic, see Imam Ahmad Raza Khan al-Qadiri's "The Parents of the exalted Prophet ﷺ are Believers" in *Thesis of Imam Ahmad Raza* (Durban: Barkaatur-Raza Publications, 2007).

[iii] The Qur'an says: *Verily, Allah and His Angels send blessings on the Prophet: O you who believe! Send blessings on him, and salute him with a worthy salutation.* (33:56) God's Messenger – may blessings and peace be upon him – said, "The closest people to me on the Day of Judgment are those who invoked the most blessings upon me" (*Sunan al-Tirmidhi*). And he said, "Whoever sends a single blessing upon me, God sends ten blessings upon him" (*Sahih Muslim*). Another narration adds: "By it God will remove from the supplicant ten sins and raise his rank ten degrees" (*Sunan al-Nasa'i*).

[iv] Shaykh 'Abd al-Qadir al-Jilani, *The Book of the Secret of Secrets and the Manifestation of Lights* (Fort Lauderdale: Al-Baz Publishing Inc., 2000), trans. Muhtar Holland, 7.

[v] This is a well-known hadith narrated by Muslim, Ahmad, and al-Tirmidhi.

[vi] As the Prophet – God bless him and give him peace – has said: "The first thing that Allah created was my spirit [*ruh*]. The first thing that Allah created was my light [*nur*]. The first thing that Allah created was the pen [*qalam*]. The first thing that Allah created was the intellect ['*aql*]." The venerable Shaykh 'Abdul Qadir al-Jilani – may God be well pleased with him – commented upon this hadith in his *The Book of the Secret of the Secrets* saying: "This means that they are all one thing, that being the Muhammadan Reality [*al-Haqiqat al-Muhammadiyya*], but it is called a 'light [*nur*]' because it is pure and unclouded by the darkness of Majesty. As Allah (Blessed and Exalted is He) has said: *There has now come to you from Allah a Light, and a clear Book.* (5:15) It is also called an 'intellect ['*aql*],' because it comprehends universal truths [*kulliyyat*]. It is also called a 'pen [*qalam*],' because it is an instrument for the transmission of knowledge, just as the pen is an instrument in the realm of letters [of

the alphabet]. The Muhammadan spirit is thus the quintessence of all entities, the first of all beings and the origin of them all."

[vii] Shaykh Monawwar Ateeq gave a very nice talk on the importance of the Messenger of God – may blessings and peace be upon him – by expounding upon one of his most beautiful Arabic names mentioned in the Munificent Qur'an, *Siraj,* which means an illuminating lamp and a shining sun (http://www.almukhtarbooks. com/?page_id=10).

[viii] Abu Hurayrah – may God be well pleased with him – reported that the Prophet – may blessings and peace be upon him – said, "I was sent from the best generation of the sons of Adam, generation by generation, until I was in the generation where I now am" (*Sahih al-Bukhari*).

[ix] The material for much of this paragraph and the one preceding it was gleamed from Dr. Martin Lings internationally acclaimed biography, *Muhammad ﷺ: His Life Based on the Earliest Sources* (Rochester: Inner Traditions, 2006), Chapters 4-7.

[x] Abu Nu'aym narrated this report on the authority of Ibn Abbas – may God be well pleased with him – in his *Dala'il al-Nabuwwah.* Cf. 'Allama Abdul Mustafa Azmi, *Muhammad ﷺ: The Prophet of Islam* (Bolton: Maktab-e-Qadriah, 2009), trans. Mawlana Omar Dawood Qadri, 14.

[xi] Lings, *Muhammad ﷺ: His Life Based on the Earliest Sources*, 21.

[xii] Azmi, *Muhammad ﷺ: The Prophet of Islam*, 7.

[xiii] Lings, *Muhammad ﷺ: His Life Based on the Earliest Sources*, 21-22.

[xiv] Azmi, *Muhammad ﷺ: The Prophet of Islam*, 14-15.

[xv] Ibid., 15.

www.ingramcontent.com/pod-product-compliance
Lightning Source LLC
Chambersburg PA
CBHW041759040426
42447CB00001B/28